PRINCETON

WASHINGTON'S CROSSING
DECEMBER 25, 1776

BATTLE OF TRENTON
DECEMBER 26, 1776

BATTLE OF PRINCETON
JANUARY 3, 1777

ASSUNPINK CREEK

Americans March to Princeton

N
W E
S

0   1   2
Miles

To my grandson, Philip Richard Perry —L. C.

For America's first patriots—through their sacrifice we live their dream —P. M. F.

Acknowledgments

My first thanks are to Peter Fiore, whose talent for painting and passion for history have helped make this heroic story come alive. I would also like to thank Elisabeth Irwin, my able research assistant, who has a keen eye for detail and a fine instinct for exactly the historical source I need. I have also been blessed with skilled editors, Brenda Bowen and Paula Wiseman, and a gifted and resourceful designer, Lee Wade. I'm also grateful to Jordan Brown, Lisa Ford, Hilary Goodman, Dorothy Gribbin, and Dan Potash, all part of a team at Simon & Schuster that turns words and pictures into lovely children's books.

I am indebted to many people who work at libraries, museums, and historical sites, including Beth Davis-Brown at the Library of Congress; Katherine Ludwig at the David Library of the American Revolution; Valerie-Anne Lutz at the American Philosophical Society Library; Michelle Matz at Washington Crossing Historic Park; Catherine S. Medich at the New Jersey State Archives; John Mills at Princeton Battlefield State Park; Wendy Nardi at Trenton Public Library; and Richard Patterson, director of the Old Barracks Museum in Trenton.

Special thanks go to David Hackett Fischer, author of many books, including the splendid *Washington's Crossing*. He not only read a draft of this book and made helpful suggestions, but he also pointed me to the account of Martha Reed, a little girl who lived in Trenton in 1776. As the grandfather of Thea, David knows what will pique a child's interest.

I want to express my gratitude to the American Enterprise Institute, in particular to its president, Chris DeMuth, who started me on this project in 2002 by lending me James T. Flexner's *George Washington in the American Revolution*. Chris supports AEI scholars with great patience and good cheer—as evidenced by the fact that he has yet to ask for his book back.

And to Bob Barnett, renowned advocate for books, I would like once again to extend my appreciation. This is the third of my children's books about American history that he has guided to publication and my third time to thank him for donating his efforts. The charitable causes that these books support benefit from his generosity. —L. C.

I would like to thank Mrs. Cheney for selecting me to create the paintings for her powerful telling of this historic event. I would like to thank the Brigade of the American Revolution and all its members who reenacted many of the actions that are in this book; David Hackett Fischer for lending his historical knowledge in helping me set the time of day for many of the paintings; the Old Barracks Museum in Trenton, New Jersey, and its director, Richard Patterson, for historical information; Michelle Matz of the Washington Crossing Historic Park in Washington Crossing, Pennsylvania, for reference and access to the reenactors of the annual crossing. Lastly, a thank-you to my son, Paul Fiore, for his additional photography and reference-gathering for me.

Again, thank you all. —P. M. F.

SIMON & SCHUSTER BOOKS FOR YOUNG READERS
An imprint of Simon & Schuster Children's Publishing Division
1230 Avenue of the Americas, New York, New York 10020
Text copyright © 2004 by Lynne Cheney
Illustrations copyright © 2004 by Peter M. Fiore
All rights reserved, including the right of reproduction
in whole or in part in any form.
SIMON & SCHUSTER BOOKS FOR YOUNG READERS
is a trademark of Simon & Schuster, Inc.
Book design by Lee Wade
The text for this book is set in Celestia Antique.
The illustrations for this book are rendered in oil paints on canvas.
Manufactured in the United States of America

10 9 8 7 6 5 4 3 2 1
Library of Congress Cataloging-in-Publication Data
Cheney, Lynne V.
When Washington crossed the Delaware : a wintertime story for young patriots /
Lynne Cheney ; illustrated by Peter Fiore.— 1st ed.
p. cm.
ISBN 0-689-87043-4
1. Trenton, Battle of, Trenton, N.J., 1776—Juvenile literature. 2. Washington,
George, 1732-1799—Juvenile literature. [1. Trenton, Battle of, Trenton, N.J., 1776.
2. United States—History—Revolution, 1775-1783—Campaigns. 3. Washington,
George, 1732-1799.] I. Fiore, Peter M., ill. II. Title.
E241.T7C47 2004   973.3'32—dc22
2003027648

George Washington's signature courtesy of Mount Vernon Ladies' Association

Editor's Note: Archaic spelling, capitalization, and punctuation in historical quotations have been modernized throughout the text.

WHEN *Washington*
CROSSED THE *Delaware*

A wintertime story for young patriots

BY

Lynne Cheney

LYNNE CHENEY

PAINTINGS BY
PETER M. FIORE

SIMON & SCHUSTER BOOKS FOR YOUNG READERS
New York   London   Toronto   Sydney

One of the tales I like to tell my grandchildren is about Washington crossing the Delaware. It's a compelling story, and it helps them understand that our existence as a free and independent nation wasn't always assured. Given the way that the Revolutionary War was going in the months leading up to Christmas 1776, the most likely outcome was that we would remain a British colony. But then George Washington and his men took history into their own hands and changed its course.

I tell my grandchildren that there was nothing easy about what these men did. Ill-equipped and poorly clothed, they made a dangerous crossing, marched through freezing weather, and twice took on the greatest army in the world. These Americans were models of persistence, but that wasn't the only thing that carried them through. They had an inspiring leader, a man who understood that his composure calmed his men and that his bravery emboldened them. Washington was also a brilliant tactician. Twice in ten days he made up for American disadvantages by wielding the weapon of surprise.

At a time of year when children have presents much on their mind, the story of Washington's crossing provides a chance to talk about a different kind of generosity. While gifts that we wrap in paper and ribbon make people happy, brave deeds that lift the spirits are a mighty force. With a campaign that began on Christmas night, Washington and his army gave their countrymen the powerful gift of hope. After the victories at Trenton and Princeton, Americans knew they could win, and this knowledge would sustain them through the years of war that lay ahead.

In 1776 twenty-four hundred men crossed the Delaware. In 2004 two hundred ninety million Americans are the beneficiaries of their bravery.

Lynne Cheney

I remember reading in my youth a small book—*The Life of Washington*—and of all his struggles none fixed itself on my mind so indelibly as the crossing of the Delaware preceding the battle of Trenton. . . . I am exceedingly anxious that the object they fought for—liberty, and the Union and Constitution they formed—shall be perpetual.

—ABRAHAM LINCOLN, *February 21, 1861*

It was November 1776, a time of trouble for our young country. We were fighting for our independence from Britain, and the war was not going well. The British had defeated General George Washington and his men on Long Island, had driven them out of New York, and were pursuing them across New Jersey.

George Washington was discouraged. How could the Americans, who were mostly new to fighting, ever hope to defeat the well-trained redcoats?

"The rebels fly before us."
WILLIAM BAMFORD
CAPTAIN, BRITISH ARMY

> *"This night we lay amongst the leaves without tents or blankets."*
>
> Enoch Anderson
> Captain, Haslet's Delaware Regiment

The Americans retreated through cold and rain. Many had no jackets to keep them warm. Many had no shoes and marched with rags wrapped around their feet. Everyone was hungry.

In early December the Americans made it across the Delaware River into Pennsylvania. Under General Washington's orders they had taken every boat they could find with them, so they knew they were safe from the British for a while. But they were sick, exhausted, and cold.

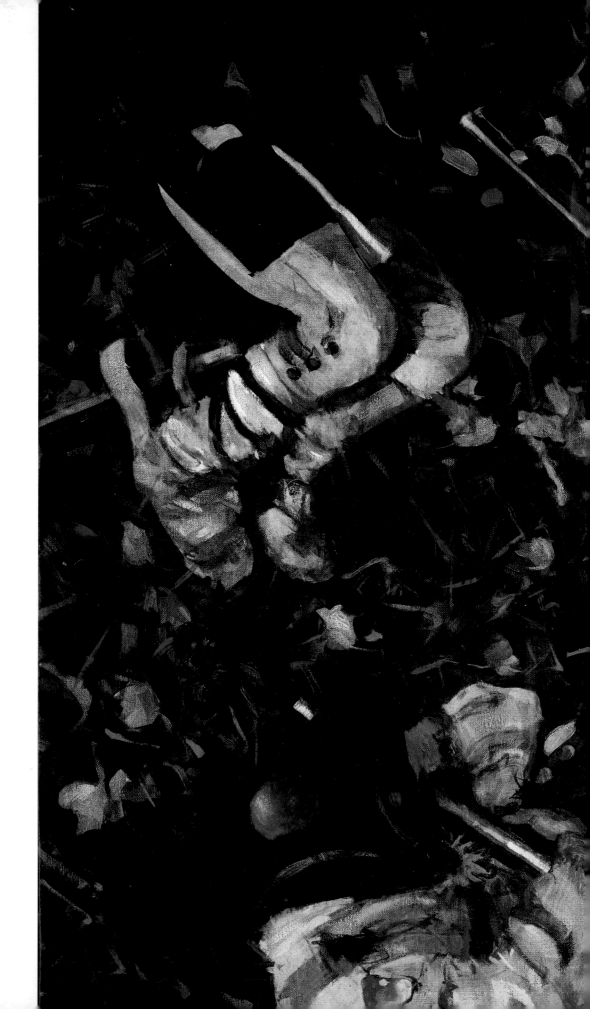

Even when the struggle seemed hopeless, George Washington did not give up. On the other side of the river the British had stationed Hessians—German soldiers the British had hired to fight for them. The Hessians didn't have much respect for American soldiers. They didn't think the Americans would do anything bold or daring—and so George Washington decided on a bold and daring course.

He called a meeting of his generals and worked out a plan. On Christmas night American troops would cross the Delaware River in several different places. Before dawn on December 26 they would attack the Hessians at Trenton, New Jersey.

Washington warned his officers to keep the plan a secret. It could only succeed, he believed, if the Americans caught the Hessians by surprise.

"Christmas day at night . . . is the time fixed upon for our attempt on Trenton."
GENERAL GEORGE WASHINGTON

> *"Let them call me rebel."*
>
> THOMAS PAINE
> WRITER AND SOLDIER

Also crucial to success was the spirit of the American troops. Beaten down as they were, could they fight another battle?

A man named Thomas Paine had marched with the Americans as they retreated across New Jersey. Now he came up with words to encourage them. "These are the times that try men's souls," he wrote. "The summer soldier and the sunshine patriot will, in this crisis, shrink from the service of their country; but he that stands it *now*, deserves the love and thanks of man and woman."

In the camps along the Delaware, George Washington's men read Paine's words and drew strength from them for the battle ahead.

On Christmas night, 1776, General Washington led twenty-four hundred men, the main body of his army, to a crossing point about nine miles upstream from Trenton. There the soldiers crowded into the large black boats that would take them to the opposite shore.

The night was cold, and the men faced a difficult crossing. They had to break through ice to get the boats into the river. They had to fend off large chunks of floating ice once they were underway.

But Washington had seafarers with him that night who knew how to navigate treacherous waters. The sailors of Massachusetts's Marblehead Battalion maneuvered boat after boat across the icy river. As soon as they got one group of men to the New Jersey shore, they returned to pick up another.

"The force of the current, the sharpness of the frost . . . , the ice which made during the operation . . . rendered the passage of the river extremely difficult."
—JAMES WILKINSON
MAJOR, CONTINENTAL ARMY

Washington arrived on the New Jersey side of the Delaware in the early hours of the crossing. Wrapped in his cloak, he watched his cold, wet soldiers make their way onto land. Their spirits were good, but he was worried. The crossing was taking longer than he had planned.

Washington's army had eighteen cannon, and getting them across the river was especially hard. A gun with its carriage and ammunition could weigh two thousand pounds, and loading it on and off a slippery ferry was slow and dangerous work.

Downstream two of Washington's commanders also struggled to get men and guns across the river. In the end neither General James Ewing nor Colonel John Cadwalader could get through the ice on the Delaware. They had to give up on the idea of fighting at Trenton.

But at three o'clock in the morning George Washington's crossing succeeded. The last gun was onshore, and the general and his men prepared for the nine-mile march to Trenton.

"Perseverance accomplished what at first seemed impossible."
HENRY KNOX
COLONEL, CONTINENTAL ARMY

*"Remember now what you are
about to fight for."*
GENERAL GEORGE WASHINGTON

It was four o'clock in the morning before the army was ready to move out, hours later than Washington had planned. He had hoped to attack the Hessians while it was still dark, but now the sun would be up before the Americans reached Trenton. Would an attack in daylight still be a surprise?

But there was no turning back. Through cold and sleet the American troops moved along icy roads toward Trenton. Washington and his officers rode alongside the men, encouraging them onward.

When the Americans encountered the first Hessians, it was clear that the surprise had worked. The startled Hessians retreated. The Americans pressed forward with such determination that the Hessians had little time to organize a defense. When American artillery began to bombard them, the German soldiers had no choice but to abandon the streets of Trenton and withdraw to an orchard nearby.

Nineteen-year-old Captain Alexander Hamilton led one of the companies firing on the Hessians. He would later sign the U.S. Constitution and help insure that the states accepted it. He would become our country's first secretary of the treasury.

Another soldier fighting that day was eighteen-year-old Lieutenant James Monroe. When the Hessians managed to get two of their cannon into operation, Monroe was one of the officers who charged the guns. He was badly wounded, but he would live to become our nation's fifth president.

"Then, in the grey dawn, came the beating of drums and the sound of firing."
MARTHA REED
A TEN-YEAR-OLD

"This is a glorious day for our country."
GENERAL GEORGE WASHINGTON

The Hessians tried an attack of their own. With drums beating they marched from the orchard toward the center of town. But the Americans were strong. In the fight that followed, the Hessian commander, Colonel Johann Rall, was mortally wounded and many of his men were killed.

The rest of the Hessians retreated, but the Americans soon had them surrounded. Two German regiments decided it was time to quit fighting, and they lowered their flags to the ground. Then the third— and last—regiment surrendered.

Two hours from the time it had started, the Battle of Trenton was over. With few losses of their own the Americans had captured nearly nine hundred Hessians. After many defeats they had won a great victory.

Most of Washington's men had the right to go home at the end of the year, but Washington needed them to stay. Persuading them to keep fighting would be hard, he knew. He could see how tired they were as they transported their Hessian prisoners across the Delaware to Pennsylvania. He could see that they were cold. Many marched without shoes and left bloody footprints in the snow.

Once his men were back in New Jersey, Washington promised extra pay to those who would serve longer. And he appealed to their love for their country. This was an hour of destiny, he told one regiment, a time that would decide America's fate. If they wanted their country to be free, they had to keep fighting.

Drums rolled. A few of the men stepped forward, then more, and then more. Many of Washington's battle-tested soldiers resolved to stay at his side.

———

"We know not how to spare you."
GENERAL GEORGE WASHINGTON

———

There were thousands of British and Hessian troops gathering at Princeton, New Jersey, a pretty college town northeast of Trenton. Certain that they would soon attack, Washington sent out a call for more forces. Veteran fighters joined him, as did many men who had never fought before.

Washington ordered most of his troops to line up along a ridge on the south side of Assunpink Creek. He also sent a force to the north side of the creek, where the British and Hessians were advancing. Washington ordered these men to slow the enemy down.

Near evening on January 2, 1777, the troops sent to delay the British had done all they could. They ran for a narrow bridge that would take them back across the Assunpink. As they crowded onto it, they saw General Washington at the far end. The enemy was right behind them, but the sight of their commander, firm and steady, gave them courage.

"I pressed against the shoulder of the General's horse and in contact with the boot of the General. The horse stood as firm as the rider."

JOHN HOWLAND
PRIVATE, LIPPITT'S RHODE ISLAND REGIMENT

General Charles Cornwallis, the British commander, thought he had Washington trapped. He thought he could wait until morning to attack the Americans.

But Washington had other plans. He knew that Cornwallis had brought most of his forces with him. That meant there would be far fewer of the enemy in Princeton, and so Washington readied his army for a march that would take them around Cornwallis's troops and toward the college town.

He ordered some of his men to stay behind. They were to keep campfires burning and to make noises with their axes and shovels so that the British wouldn't realize what the Americans were doing.

About one o'clock in the morning on January 3, Washington and the main body of his army moved out. Cannon wheels were muffled with rags. Officers whispered orders. The Americans did everything they could to be quiet, and their plan worked. It was dawn before Cornwallis realized they were gone.

"[Colonel] Fitzgerald, horror-struck at the danger of his beloved commander, . . . drew his hat over his face that he might not see him die."

GEORGE WASHINGTON PARKE CUSTIS
GRANDSON OF MARTHA WASHINGTON

The morning was clear and cold as Washington and his men neared Princeton. In farmland outside the town a part of the American army encountered British troops. During the fight that followed, many of the Americans fell. The dazed survivors retreated.

Washington rushed to rally his troops, and astride a white horse he led them forward, taking them to within thirty yards of the British line. American muskets were pointed at the British. British arms were leveled at the Americans. Washington was in between. Once the two sides started firing, it seemed impossible that he would survive.

Muskets roared, but when the smoke cleared, General Washington was safe. His troops held steady, but the British line broke and fell back.

The Americans advanced. British officers tried to rally the redcoats, but soon they began to flee. When the American troops ran after them, Washington paused just long enough to give a few orders. Then, spurring his horse, he joined in the pursuit.

Within a few hours the battle was over. George Washington and his men had once again defeated the greatest military power in the world.

"Away, my dear colonel, and bring up the troops—the day is our own."
GENERAL GEORGE WASHINGTON
TO COLONEL JOHN FITZGERALD

*G*eneral Washington and his men

had stood with their country in a time of crisis.

When they were cold and hungry, they did not quit. When the

conflict was hard, they fought on.

And when they won, the victory was sweet.

News of Trenton and Princeton spread across the land,

lifting the spirits of patriots everywhere.

Many a battle lay ahead, but now Americans could think

of winning their war for independence.

Now they could imagine that their

great struggle would have a glorious end.

Sources

How do we know what we know about the past? Parents and teachers who want to discuss this question with children may find the sources below a useful starting point. They range from diary entries written at the time events happened, to memories recorded at a later date, to a comment that has been repeated so often, it has become part of the tradition surrounding the campaign that began on Christmas 1776.

"I remember reading in my youth a small book . . ."
Lincoln's words, spoken at the statehouse in Trenton, were recorded in New Jersey Senate Journals of February 21, 1861.

"The rebels fly before us."
William Bamford described the fleeing Americans in his diary on November 23, 1776. The diary was published in *Maryland Historical Magazine* in 1932 and 1933.

"This night we lay amongst the leaves . . ."
Enoch Anderson reported on the suffering of the American soldiers in a series of letters he wrote to his nephew after the Revolutionary War. The letters were published as *Personal Recollections of Captain Enoch Anderson* (Wilmington: The Historical Society of Delaware, 1896).

"Christmas day at night . . . is the time fixed . . ."
General Washington wrote of his plans in a letter to Colonel Joseph Reed on December 23, 1776. His letter can be found in William S. Stryker's book *The Battles of Trenton and Princeton* (1898; reprint, Trenton, New Jersey: Old Barracks Association, 2001).

"Let them call me rebel."
Thomas Paine's words are from the first of a series of essays he wrote called *The American Crisis*. This essay was published in Philadelphia on December 19, 1776.

"The force of the current, the . . ."
James Wilkinson wrote this description in *Memoirs of My Own Times* (1816; reprint, New York: AMS Press, 1973).

"Perseverance accomplished what . . ."
Henry Knox's description is from a letter to his wife written on December 28, 1776. His letter can be found in William S. Stryker's *The Battles of Trenton and Princeton*. Knox served as secretary of war when George Washington was president.

"Remember now what you are . . ."
George Washington's words are reported in William S. Stryker's *The Battles of Trenton and Princeton*.

"Then, in the grey dawn, came the beating . . ."
Martha Reed, who married John Shannon when she grew up, told her grandchildren about her experiences at the Battle of Trenton. Her granddaughter, Susan Pindar Embury, wrote down Martha Reed Shannon's memories in "A Grandmother's Recollections of the Old Revolutionary Days," an unpublished essay that can be found in the Trenton Public Library in Trenton, New Jersey.

"This is a glorious day for our country."
Washington's words were reported by James Wilkinson in *Memoirs of My Own Times*.

"We know not how to spare you."
Washington's words were reported by a soldier known only as Sergeant R., who recorded his memories many years after these events. They were published in *The Phenix* on March 24, 1832, and were reprinted in *Pennsylvania Magazine of History and Biography* in 1896.

"I pressed against the shoulder of the . . ."
John Howland's words are from a description he wrote that was first published in 1831. It was published again in a book called *Thirty Days in New Jersey Ninety Years Ago* (Trenton, New Jersey: State Gazette Office, 1867).

"We've got the old fox safe now. We'll go . . ."
Cornwallis's boast has become a part of the tradition surrounding the battles of Trenton and Princeton. This particular version is from James Thomas Flexner's *George Washington in the American Revolution (1775–1783)* (Boston: Little, Brown, 1967). Flexner notes that Cornwallis is "reputed" to have uttered these words.

The redcoats pictured elsewhere in this book are British regulars. This soldier keeping watch is a light infantryman.

"[Colonel] Fitzgerald, horror-struck at . . ."
George Washington Parke Custis, Martha Washington's grandson, whom George and Martha Washington raised as their son, told Colonel John Fitzgerald's story in *Recollections and Private Memoirs of Washington* (New York: Derby and Jackson, 1860).

"Away, my dear colonel, and bring up . . ."
George Washington's words are reported in George Washington Parke Custis's *Recollections*.

PLAN OF THE OPERATIONS
OF GENERAL WASHINGTON
AGAINST THE KING'S TROOPS

from the 25th of December 1776 to the 3rd of January 1777

WASHINGTON CROSSES
THE DELAWARE

Americans March to Trenton

NEW JERSEY

DELAWARE RIVER
full of ice

PENNSYLVANIA

TRENTON